THE ILLUMINATI

Conspiracy Theories Surrounding The Secret Cult's Laws, History And Operations – Where's The Truth?

Seth Balfour

LIKE FREE BOOKS?

Would you like them delivered to you every week?

Do you like non-fiction books on a huge range of different topics?

We send out FREE e-books every week so we can share our books with the world!

We have FREE books every week on AMAZON that we send to our email list.

So if you want in, then visit the link at the end of this book to sign up and sit back and wait for new books to be sent straight to your inbox!

TABLE OF CONTENTS

Introduction

Conclusion

INTRODUCTION

The Illuminati is a cult you've definitely heard of before. Not because of their heavy influence or the power they had over history, but due to something that's much harder to understand and comprehend...

Internet memes. Jokes. Someone makes a video and adds the iconic pyramid with an eye from the American one-dollar bill to it and creepy music on top of it, posts it on YouTube with a title that goes something like "THE ILLUMINATI ARE BEHIND FACEBOOK!" and in come the views and comments.

The number of these jokes online is incredibly high, all of which are easier to find than actual information about what the Illuminati were about, what they've done or why they existed, if they still exist at all.

There is another group of people that have an interest in the Illuminati, those being fanatics. People who proclaim that they were nothing less than the servants of Satan himself. Their ultimate goal? To take over every known government and prepare the world for the return of none other than Antichrist.

You could go with either of these groups, one that takes said cult as nothing but a silly joke, or the other, which thinks of it as one of the most evil and satanic groups in history. All of this begs the question...

What is the real story behind the Illuminati? Where does it start? How did it end? And, most importantly, did it end at all? Is this elusive group still having meetings to this day, planning and scheming behind everyone's backs?

Where is the truth in their story, and can we find it? Yes.

But to get to the meat of it, the unfiltered truth behind the Illuminati, we first have to go back to 1776, when their story starts. Our location? Bavaria...

CHAPTER 1

ADAM WEISHAUPT – THE FOUNDER

Adam Weishaupt is the man it all started with. If you've never heard of Adam before, he's the man solely responsible for the start of the Illuminati movement. Let's explore his tale in more detail.

His father died when he was just five years old, and his mother? Nobody knows what happened to her. After his father's death he was raised and heavily influenced by his grandfather, who had some very strong rationalist beliefs.

Rationalist beliefs? Don't forget, we traveled back more than 200 years for this. Rationalism, reading this in the 21st century, should sound like a pretty good idea to most people. What's being rational? Being realistic, calm, calculative, which sounds pretty good...

Sadly, the way reality works is, nothing is as good as it sounds at first. Rationalists believed that truth can be quantified. That there are things in this world that simply cannot, under any circumstance, be denied, proved false.

You might be thinking, that's kind of true. For example, everyone has to die eventually, the Earth is flat and so on and so forth. Well, that's not how they really saw it. Their actual belief was that our whole reality works under a certain logical system.

A hidden, out of sight mechanism which can be grasped by our minds, if we care enough to see it, which ironically, doesn't sound rational. That's what Adam's grandfather left him with, his beliefs and some very interesting ideas and education.

Adam seemed to take this to heart and in May of 1776, he founded the Bavarian Illuminati, naming himself Brother Spartacus. Now, why did I point out that it was Bavarian? Well, it's very important to understand a few things about what the word itself, not the cult, means throughout history. It's impact and weight.

First off, albeit it's a bit childish, it's a very cool sounding name for an organization. It really makes it sound like this group, whatever it may be about, is important and is about to make some important revelations that you should really pay attention to.

And, as with all things that are considered cool, the title of the Illuminati has been reused hundreds of times since it first showed up. These days, the word is used as a blanket term for a secret society that's ran by THE ELITE. You'd be surprised by how many famous actors are said to be a part of it.

It might actually be true, as famous actors being a part of the Illuminati sounds ridiculous enough that people just might ignore it and dismiss it as nothing but a joke. And let's not put aside those movies, video games, books and myths where the Illuminati turn out to be real all along and, in a shocking twist, they're also ruling the world. A very common story in modern media.

Some of these works, if not most, are supposed to be fully fictional of course, just using the cool name to poke at people's interest. But there is a pretty significant amount of works which are absolutely serious about the Illuminati running the world, controlling wars and governments, even to this day. That everything around us is shaped by them, those few in great power.

Just the implication that those powerful few have so much power is incredibly hard to resist thinking about. But, we're spending too much time in 2016, and we're not even done with 1776.

Let's go back to Adam's story. So what was Adam's goal? It's a great question, but if you think this or any other book will give you a factual answer to that, you're wasting your time.

The history of the Bavarian Illuminati, their true goals and operations are covered in so many lies that telling the truth apart from myth is borderline impossible. This probably wasn't the work of their genius to throw us off their trail, but is a simple by-product of our societies obsession with them. The truth is buried deep, facts are muddled and years have passed, making the process of recovery rather difficult.

Although numerous books offer you the answer to many of the burning questions about the Illuminati, I'm sad to inform you that the truth isn't that clear cut when it comes to this subject.

At some points, when you read about the Illuminati, you have to accept that most, if not all of it, is lies. The goal of the Bavarian Illuminati is still a bit of a mystery to this day, but it'd be more accurate to say that time has damaged our clarity on the matter.

I said a bit of a mystery for a good reason. We do know more than a few things about them, some in high detail. Their Illuminating beliefs, their founder's history, a few of their basic rules as well. Even with all of that in our hands, the full picture is blurred, it's missing pieces, lies and myths taking their place.

There are more than a few theories about what their ultimate goal was, of course. One fits with Adams rationalist beliefs at the time, that he formed it with peace and illumination as his ultimate goal. Peace where? Peace everywhere.

Adams ambition is something worth admiring, but it does make you wonder how he thought he could accomplish something like that.

To start him off, Adam needed one thing the most. Recruits. Fresh blood to join his cult, help it grow and expand faster. It is believed that the cult started off with just five people. Adam had never ran a cult before, but he was smart enough to know you can't run a cult that has influence without having plentiful members.

He had it all planned out, he managed to join the Masonic Lodge in 1777 with the goal of poking peoples interest into his own cult. It worked, and his Illuminati grew. It grew so much in fact, that he caught the attention of the Elector of Bavaria, Charles Theodore, a name you should remember, as he plays a major role in not just the fate of the Bavarian Illuminati, but Adam's as well.

The Bavarian Illuminati were against laws and societies being built based on any religion or tradition and that everything should be based on rationalism, undeniable truth and logic. His words and ideals were said to be too radical and extreme for the time to lead anywhere good.

Whoever said that was right on the money, because in 1785, Charles Theodore disbanded the Bavarian Illuminati and also exiled Adam from Bavaria. Adam was lucky enough to be assisted by the Duke Ernest, who let him and his family stay in Gotha. He stayed there, living with his family until 1830, when he passed away.

He was buried next to his son.

The Illuminati movement was banned, its leader exiled and dead. Most members moved on, went on to do other things, some of them doing things which Adam and his Illuminating beliefs would not approve of.

So what happened to the Bavarian Illuminati after they were banned? Nothing, it would appear. There simply is not any hard proof that the movement continued its existence after the ban, yet alone that they're still active to this day.

This is something some might call hitting the wall. It's what happens to everyone who investigates the illuminati, they eventually hit it and it's very discouraging. There just isn't much information to go on after

1785, and even from 1776 to 1785, there isn't that much.

What did they talk about during their meetings? What did they discuss in them? Did they influence any events in the period we know they were active in? If so, how and why? Why did Adam call himself Brother Spartacus? Did all members have nicknames?

We simply do not know. There are only myths and rumors, many of which you have probably heard at some point. When someone talks of the Illuminati, literally anything is a possibility.

9/11? Illuminati were behind it! World War II? The Illuminati were behind it! The French revolution? Guess who?

They could be behind all of those events and behind everything behind those events. They are, and have been for so many years, a scapegoat for a reason behind any major event. They're every conspirator's dream, fitting all the criteria.

An awesome name. Existing for hundreds of years, operating silently from the shadows. Plotting, scheming their next big move. Why and how? Those questions don't matter. It's the events that do.

If you believe some people, they were behind so many historical events that their powers can be described as nothing but godly. And it is exactly these historical events, events of blood, of unimaginable terror, fear and torment, that we are going to explore right now...

CHAPTER 2

THEIR REVOLUTION

You will notice a very peculiar consistency if you look into events that were supposedly orchestrated by the Illuminati. All of these events were awful. They usually involve the death of innocence, war, bloodshed and similar horrors. This is what most of them have in common.

You will never hear, in your life, someone saying: "I think the Illuminati STOPPED World War II!" or anything like that. That's something you should keep in mind as we go over the many allegations against them.

For this segment, I'll mostly focus on one of the most horrific events that they supposedly caused, and it is just one of many on the list.

The French Revolution

There isn't a better way to start off any list. The French Revolution is one of the most violent, bloody and tense historical events in our whole history, but many other events fit that description as well. What makes this one so special, is how it relates to the beliefs of the Bavarian Illuminati, and how it happened only several years after their supposed ban.

It's important to understand how brutal the French Revolution truly was. Imagine this scene. It's 1789. You're in France. And everywhere around you, as far as the eye can see, fire.

Smoke and fire everywhere you look, spreading across the city.

There are people running around, into each other, over each other, directionless. They're setting houses on fire, fighting each other, stealing, screaming. Some people on the street help the soldiers in blue to fight the ones in red uniforms, but are cut down swiftly.

Countless people died. Streets all over France were filled with blood and corpses that kept on piling up. Blood ran through the streets. Numerous executions happened daily, all done by a guillotine. Bodies piling up, cities burning. Innocent people getting executed, one after another, with no end in sight.

This was a time of absolute terror and insanity. The ending to this chaos is fitting. The king himself was eventually executed by a guillotine, and so was his wife. She paid dearly for the blade of the guillotine to be sharp, to ensure both her and her husband have quick and painless deaths.

The French Revolution would be a talked about event for centuries even if that was all there was to it. But that was just the start of it. Its conclusion affected the whole world and was one of the first steps towards the kind of world we live in today.

It started the slow but certain abolishment of monarchies all over the world, which spawned countless other wars, wars so great and impactful that they changed the world forever. The French Revolution wasn't just a revolution and a change for France, but for the entire world as well.

There's no denying that this event, more than any other in our history, has shaped the world we live in today. There were many reasons behind it of course. Nothing that gigantic comes out of nowhere.

But one of the reasons behind it, or principles you could say, was

Enlightenment. What is it? Just a philosophical movement which pushed the concepts such as liberty and freedom, while challenging the idea that religions should dictate laws and the government.

Which does sound familiar.

This was one of the core beliefs of the Bavarian Illuminati. But wait a second, didn't the Bavarian Illuminati cease to exist a few years before the revolution happened?

Can it be true? That they were the real reason behind it? Did they influence the globe with their subtle, yet effective brainwashing, getting them ready for a brand new world, built in their vision?

No.

Don't get me wrong, it's an incredibly story, but the amount of influence, power, time and planning needed is absurd. "But that's the thing about the Illuminati!" - says a hypothetical conspiracy theorist. "They're so powerful that we don't even know!" – he goes on.

One of the main reasons why people get into the idea of some secret powerful cult being behind these events, is that it's literally impossible to disapprove the Illuminati not being behind them.

It might sound like a joke, but it isn't. Can you or I or anyone else prove, with absolute certainty that they weren't behind the French revolution? Behind 9/11? Behind Brexit?

To best show how this argument usually plays out, I'll present it in a form of a text chat between two people. Zack and John will be our characters. Which one is on which side will be very obvious.

Zack: The Illuminati were behind the French Revolution.

John: Do you have any evidence to support that?

Zack: No.

John: Why would you think they're behind it then?

Zack: Because they're the Illuminati, of course there's no evidence. They're not that stupid.

John: What else were they behind then?

Zack: Lots of things, let's see, every war that ever happened after 1785, 9/11, the media brainwashing us…

John: That sounds a bit absurd Zack… I'm not so sure they were behind any of that. Or that they exist at all in fact.

Zack: Can you prove they don't?

And then it goes in circles, no need to keep going. The logic employed here is that, just because there's no evidence of something being true or real, it doesn't mean it isn't. This makes arguing against John rather pointless and exhausting, as it's an argument you simply cannot beat.

So I won't waste time doing that, when we have more than four hundred years of history supposedly shaped by the Illuminati to go through. So what else did they do, besides shaping everything to their will?

If you plan on googling the events that they orchestrated, I'll save you some time. It's very simple and easy to find out if the Illuminati were behind an event. Look for these clues.

-The event you're thinking of is wildly known

-Its outcome shook the world

-The event caused immense suffering

Those seem to be the requirements people check before calling something a part of the Illuminati conspiracy. And this wouldn't be a book worthy of its name if we didn't cover some of the most famous ones. Let's get started.

..

CHAPTER 3

YOU'RE EITHER WITH THEM OR DEAD

The subtitle says it all.

One of the most popular Illuminati theories after the French Revolution is nothing more than the death of two brothers. That might sound underwhelming, until you learn these brothers are John F. and Robert Kennedy.

The assassination of John F. Kennedy is so popular that it warrants a book about conspiracies surrounding it on its own, and in this hypothetical book, the Illuminati would surely be mentioned as one of the forces behind it.

The presidency of Kennedy was a wild ride for him, as much as it was for the rest of the world, mostly because it took place in the middle of the Cold War. A time of such discomfort and mass hysteria that almost nothing in recent history comes close.

Waking up every day, going to work, kissing your wife, seeing your kids go to school, trying to live a normal life. All while the looming threat of a nuclear war hangs above your head.

Whether you were Russian, American or from anywhere else, the pressure was there and it had years to build up. The Cold war was, since its first second, a war of hesitation. Both sides had each other in plain sight, aiming for absolute destruction of the other. Both triggers half pulled. Both doomsday devices loaded, ready to fire at any second.

This was, according to many conspiracy theorists, something the Illuminati wanted to trigger. They wanted the nuclear bombs to launch, they wanted Russia or America dead and buried. Either would do, as that would mean uniting the world under one new and powerful government would be easier, with only one major force to worry about.

Russia and America were the big boys of the time, and one of them had to be rid of if the Illuminati wanted their plans to progress. This brings us back to John F. Kennedy, who was working with the Illuminati, if you're to believe the rumours. And he also knew the outcome they wanted.

They wanted him to storm Russia, take down Castro for good and make sure Russia never recovered. Why would Kennedy do this? Why would he listen to such a zealous institution? Did they force him, or did he agree with their ideals?

Whether he agreed with their plans at first or not, they gave him some good reasons to listen either way. There were two sides to it. One was that, in the event he does go ahead and submit to their demands, he wouldn't just be safe from their wrath, but also ensure safety for Kennedy's for generations.

One of the things that gets thrown around is that the Bush presidents did just that. That they were loyal to the Illuminati cause, ensuring that they'd have wealth and power for generations to come. We can guess that Kennedy wasn't as knowledgeable about what the secret cult is capable of, as he went against their plans for the future.

This was their threat, but considering we're talking about the Illuminati, I should call it a promise. If he disobeyed them and dealt with Russia peacefully they would:

-Ensure that no Kennedy would ever have a chair in the White house

-Make sure his family lost their influence and power

-Eliminate him

In 1963, president Kennedy was assassinated with a bolt action sniper rifle while cruising through the streets of Dallas. His brain splattered all over the car, his wife right next to him. His assassin's name was Lee Harvey Oswald, who denied his crime, saying he was a coward that couldn't shoot anyone, yet alone the president.

This is one of the best pulled off operations by the Illuminati, according to theorists. So many other conspiracy theories spawned around the assassination that the Illuminati one was just another tiny cog in the wheel, blending in with the rest.

The strangest thing is how this seemingly simple killing was so hard to crack and to this day, no one is completely sure of what happened.

There were, since day one, theories of another shooter somewhere. Who and why? That's the tricky part. Evidence suggests that the bullet came from a different angle, one that's seemingly impossible to pull off from where Oswald was.

Asking Oswald himself seems like a great idea, but there's one little obstacle in the way of that happening. Death.

Killed two days after getting arrested, while being transferred to a different police station, by a man called Jack Ruby, who shot him, live on TV across the globe.

Will we ever know the full story behind one of the most talked about assassination's in history? We can stay hopeful, but probably not. And yet, the truth, no matter how deep they bury or hide it, is out there, somewhere. Laying peaceful, until someone digs it up.

We're not done with the Kennedy's and neither were the Illuminati. One wasn't enough.

Five years after his brother's life was taken, Robert Kennedy was also assassinated. Shot three times from a high calibre revolver by a man called Sirhan Bishara. Unlike his brother, Robert didn't die right away. He was heavily wounded though. He wasn't going to make it. A boy walked up to him as he lay on the ground, putting a rosary in his hand.

Kennedy, losing consciousness, asked him one thing. Is everyone okay? The boy said yes. Robert was taken to a hospital and died the next morning. Unlike his predecessor, this Kennedy killer is actually still alive, still serving his sentence in California. And Sirhan has a lot to say...

Every five years a parole hearing is held for Sirhan. The main reason as to why he was never released is that, quoting the parole officers, he still doesn't fully understand the weight of the crime he committed.

So what does Sirhan say in these hearings, if not that he knows what he's done and that he's sorry? He talks of being lead on by a pretty woman. Being at a party. Of getting hypnotized. Lifting a gun up and down in a hotel room. Drinking.

Prison records say that he spent hours with psychologists, just to try and restore his memory of the killing. He said the first thing he remembers clearly is being held down on the ground by two people, which was right after he shot Robert Kennedy. What could this be?

Did Sirhan jump on the conspiracy train just to justify his actions? Is he trying to fool us? Or maybe even fool himself, to not feel guilt over his crime? Both could be true, but the final possible truth is what interests us. That he is telling us the truth. That he was hypnotized, lead on and used as a puppet.

That's where his story would end, if not for the man called Paul Schrade, one of the men who witnessed the assassination first hand. Schrade's statement was that Sirhan was just a decoy, a distraction, and that the real killer was never caught. Keep in mind that mister Schrade is close to a hundred years old, but still, his statement stands. Why stand up for a killer and a man who nearly killed you alongside his target?

His target... Seems we can't be so sure about that anymore. There is an interesting pattern to be noticed in these two supposedly unconnected assassinations. Something they have in common and also something that's still not completely clear to this day.

A second shooter. In the first assassination, this is something that's discussed to this day, and for the second, it just recently came up. Sirhan swears he was hypnotized to do it, while Lee never had a chance to make such statements. One thing he did say though, is that he was a coward. That he wouldn't be able to kill anyone.

Would Lee, given time, also go down Sirhan's route? Talking of being hypnotized and used as a decoy? Two men, both claiming to be hypnotized to kill one Kennedy each in a spawn of only a few years? That would be quite the reveal.

Too bad one of their stories we will never know in full detail. It would seem our enlightened overlords are always one step ahead of us. Ahead, and above...

The Moon Landing

The world would have you believe we landed on the moon in 1969, but that is also another event the Illuminati altered to suit their needs, so some conspirators believe. They deceive again, in the most cunning of ways.

If you thought the next line you were going to read was going to be "WE NEVER LANDED ON THE MOON! IT WAS ALL RECORDED IN A STUDIO!" – you'd be dead wrong. Not only do some theorists say we did land on the moon for real, we also landed on the moon ten years earlier. And it wasn't America that did it, but Russia.

Let's look deeper into this. Russians went to space first and were years, if not decades ahead in space technology advancements compared to Americans. So how did America manage to outrun them in the landing race? One of the answers to that is quite simple.

They didn't.

Conspirators said that the landing was kept under wraps and hidden from the public by the Illuminati, who were working for both sides, with neither America or Russia knowing they were getting played by the ominous cult. So what would be their reason for setting this up? It's more genius than you'd think.

By letting America be the first on the moon officially, they were feeding the American beast even more confidence cake. Winning the Moon race made them more cocky and unpredictable, while Russia was left feeling jealous and beaten, also unpredictable.

All of that, in the middle of the Cold war. The Illuminati were throwing wood on both fires, just to keep the tension between these two giants going, in the mostly subtle of ways. All the while they knew both sides had enough nuclear bombs stockpiled to destroy not only each other, but also the rest of the world with them.

And it is this exact reason why Kennedy and his brother were assassinated...apparently. John F. Kennedy stopped something that the Illuminati were building towards for decades. Instead of waging war, president Kennedy approached Russia with more peaceful intentions, going against the cults will.

Their plan almost came to fruition. And what happened to the man stopping them from seeing it through to the end? He got his brains blown out shortly after. His family will never gain any political power ever again. His brother was assassinated as well.

The Illuminati weren't just punishing the Kennedy's for their treason, they were also making a point. Sending a message. Don't mess with us. Or we'll mess with you.

Sadly, that message doesn't seem to matter much, when their intention seems to be to mess us all up in the end anyways

...

CHAPTER 4

THE DISEASE SPREADS

Assassinations should be a very expected part of the Illuminati business. Eliminating the competition and those unwilling to support your brand new vision for the world is nothing out of character from such an organization.

Their ambitions don't seem to be that small though, which is fitting for a cult this talked about. Experimentation is another branch the Illuminati take part in, and not just any experimentation.

Virus experimentation.

Although virus engineering would be more accurate, and also more terrifying.

Some people suggest that they've been trying to perfect a virus that could wipe the entirety of the world's population in a blink, for decades. This was on their list of priorities for a long while, (apparently) and they did do test runs before.

On people. Some people attribute the world's most dangerous virus infections to them. They haven't managed to perfect it yet, as humanity did survive what they've been throwing at it, but only so far.

Who knows how many years it'll take them to make a virus that's perfect at killing us. There've been recent reports of some animals acting strange and aggressive in Brazil and Mexico, really 'under the hood stuff', but it is happening. Maybe they're using animals as guineapigs instead of us, for now...

The animals seem to be test subjects for whatever it is they're cooking up next. Let's hope we can handle it, whatever it may be. We might be able to deal with viruses, but how good are we at dealing with floods, hurricanes and earthquakes?

That's right, they can control that too. This ability is usually attributed to a machine called the HAARP. The existence of HAARP is no secret and neither is its purpose, which is to analyze the ionosphere. HAARP is just used as a convenient thing to point out as a device that can cause natural disasters at will, and it seems to be just that. Another easy scapegoat.

The only location where this machine could be located is the only one you can't see clearly from Google Maps, and there's only one place like that. Deep, under the sea. Some say the Pacific, some say the Atlantic. Wherever it is, it's down there, somewhere, so they say...

And down there, in the depths of the endless ocean, an underground base sits, housing this monstrous weapon of mass distruction.

Scientists roam its hauls, working, making sure the beast is ready for whenever its masters need its powers again. Which place is its next target? What sort of disaster will hit it? Somebody knows.

There are also rumors circling around that they were the ones who took Nikola Tesla's blueprints after his passing. If you weren't aware, Nikola was such a passionate genius that he never stopped inventing, even after he changed the world with his inventions forever. He had much grander plans for this world.

Some say free energy. Some say he built machines with such destructive power he destroyed them out of fear of what others might do with them. But did he destroy the blueprints? Blueprints which could be in the hands of the world's most dangerous cult? We can only hope that Nikola was as good at burning paper, as he was at making sparks fly.

There is another terrifying device they might have. One that doesn't just kill and destroy, but ends everything...

That's right, not even the Sun seems to be out of their reach. They apparently developed a beam which could potentially shut off the Sun itself, causing eternal darkness.

You're probably thinking to yourself, why would the Illuminati need all these powerful weapons? Their goal is to unite the whole world in peace, under one government. So why would they need all of those weapons of absolute destruction?

Because the best way to ensure total peace is fear. Fear of plagues, fear of earthquakes that flatten countries, fear of endless darkness. This is their will. If you don't like living in absolute peace, you best get ready to not live. At all.

But it's not like they're real. Right...?

CHAPTER 5

THE ASSUMED ILLUMINATI RULES

So what is this new world they're building? What would its rules, laws and morals be like? Peace being the only requirement isn't very logical, so there must be more. If we go by their actions from before, we can easily conclude that they wouldn't stand for any sort of rebellion against their vision for the world.

Which is ironic, considering that one of their original goals was to unchain the world from its intolerant ideals and monarchs. It's okay to do and say anything, except wage war and oppose your new rulers.

Again, their must be more to their vision, but we'll never know for sure until it happens, and let's hope it never does. But what of their own, internal rules? What does it take to join their ranks, to discuss and dictate the future of the world? Let's look over what their rules would probably look like.

-There is a God, of that I am sure. Of what, why and when, I do not know.

The first requirement would be to believe in some form of higher power. Which basically means, you accept that there is a being greater than us, one that created the world. The Illuminati cults all over the world in the present, also enforce this rule, but more on them later.

-Men below me and above me are all equal in my eyes. They are no greater or less great than I, nor am I.

Another rule is to never gloat. Never show off your wealth or power during the meetings themselves. That power and wealth comes in play outside of them of course, making operations possible. It's safe to assume they wore some kind of masks, as it fits with their goal of purging humanity of all governments and believing in enlightenment. Maybe they would try to support the notion of equality by the gesture.

-I shan't speak of this. I shan't remember this. What this is, is nothing. We are not real. We do not exist.

A very simple, but one of the most important rules. In order for them to pull their plans off, they have to stay in the shadows. They have to stay hidden from interest and prying eyes. People must believe they are a myth, a joke. So when they strike, it's a strike no one will see coming. And when we do, it shall be too late.

-I give unto you my life, soul, wisdom and body. You are my everything, while I am nothing. I do not live with you for my happiness, I live for you, because I am compelled.

A rule about enlightenment and the path the Illuminati have chosen. A reminder of how to follow their cause accordingly. Although you'll find that it's never that easy in practice.

-I follow you for this world. All for this world. For all of its people. The rich, the poor, the young and the old. They need a saviour, and it is upon us to deliver their salvation.

A reminder of why they do what they do. Everything they do, they're doing in the interest of humanity, trying to save us from governments, monarchs and wars.

-Unite the world for you, under one watchful eye. The eye that judges the noble man just as harshly as the peasant. In its eyes, all people are equal and no man is king.

Their ambition to monitor the world and ensure equality. Moving on.

-Peace be upon us all.

The final rule, putting all of us, the whole of humanity under one roof. A roof of peace. Forced, uncomfortable peace, where no man is free to live his own way. And where the only way is the one set in stone by them.

Again, nothing is mentioned of the rules they would set up, just that they would. I guess we don't get a say in the matter.

So what if someone happens to like the rules I listed? What if they're getting on their side? What if someone wants to join them? In case someone does, they can join THE ELITE, but it will take a lot of work.

A lifetime of mustering up a fortune of billions of dollars, building up a repertoire of influential friends and showing them the right attitude, they just might become one of the few that dictate our fates.

But until then, they're just one of the puppets. You and I reader, we are not so unalike. We both try. We both live, breath, eat and sleep. And we're both looking into one of the world's most secretive and dangerous organizations. Let's just hope they're not looking into us. For both our sakes.

CHAPTER 6

NO MORE ROOM IN HELL

Satan is behind it all, is another popular theory behind the cult.

That their preaching about equality and Enlightenment is nothing but a show. But some details don't fit. Why would the world's most secretive cult have a need for that?

To have a reputation for their organization operating a certain way, no matter how vague, is very strange. You could say it's pointless, as they work in secret anyway. But there might be one good reason for it. Maybe they know that most people wouldn't be on board with working for Satan.

It's the perfect cover. The story behind this conspiracy is that Satan, out of ideas and strength to conquer humanity, was inspired by humanities begging for help, mercy and salvation. The idea was, he was going to come to Earth, disguised. Out of sight, out of reach of God.

If he is not to destroy us with his army of darkness, he would use something just as dark and evil to do it. Ourselves.

Satan, if we go by what theorists tell us, came to Earth donning skin of a regular person. A wolf in sheep's clothing. He would then, without us suspecting it, slowly grow in power over many centuries. Building up a new legion, but this one of our world.

He would manipulate us over the years, growing his influence and power without us even paying attention, because he grew that wealth and power over time. Over the years he would "change his skin" to a new, younger one.

His disguises grow old, but it's always him in charge, he's just changing skins, changing faces when need be. Not even his closest men know his secret or know of his plan. Not even the cult he started thousands of years ago know what they've been doing all this time.

Helping him get a stronger grasp on our world, and then, when his fist is clenched strong enough, he can crush it. The Illuminati organizations that came before the Bavarian didn't bear the name of the Illuminati, they weren't know by any names.

Their secrecy was easy to keep in those ages. But in this day and age, I think you can see how keeping a massive organization a secret is impossible. Anyone can monitor anything easily, find out things that are hidden in the most perfect of ways.

And this is the genius part of Satan's plan. What if, to make sure his organization doesn't fall, he announced it to the world? Years before advanced technology, Satan knew what was coming, and he had to act fast. We're jumping back to 1776, revisiting Adam Weishaupt's story.

He's about to start the Illuminati movement, inspired by his grandfather. Or so we were lead to believe. Strange how there are no records of Adam's mother. Or Adam's grandmother either.

Actually, a lot of what is known about Adam and his life seems to be too basic and convenient. Satan might have just made Adam up, just so people have someone to point at when talking about the Illuminati creator, when his existence was just a ruse.

The other possibility is that his story is true, but that he was a pawn. A puppet that was strung along and psychologically pushed into starting the Illuminati movement. His father just happens to die from an infection so he has to live with a grandfather who he's never seen or met before?

And this grandfather of his just happens to believe in these illuminating ideals? Adam was nothing more than another scapegoat. He was to think he was starting a new movement of his own, when his only purpose was to expose it to the world briefly.

He became a nuisance quickly. Maybe Satan thought this distraction was enough to keep Adam's Illuminati in people's minds for years. Something people would jump to blame and point as a source of evil and otherworldly power, when in reality, Satan was here thousands of years before, doing the exact same thing, just not in public.

If this was his intention, it worked perfectly. The Bavarian Illuminati took all the heat as the boogeyman group that controls the world, while whatever schemes he had, remained in the shadows. Out of our sight, out of our minds.

The true, real Illuminati conspiracy is not the one of uniting the world under one government.

Not one of history being manipulated by the elite for the greater Enlighted good. It's not a story of our worlds beliefs or perspectives. The Illuminati might just be a part of a bigger scheme, and just a tiny part of it. Just like the Kennedy assassinations, there seem to be two shooters. One that did it, and one that we were given to blame.

The real story behind the Illuminati is not about the Illuminati. It's a story of genius deceit. A story of unavoidable destruction. Of powers so great we're nothing to them. If that's true, we're not ready for what's coming, and if we don't open our eyes soon, we never will be.

CHAPTER 7

THE ILLUMINATI AND INTERNET MEMES

I hope you're excited for some actual facts. The truth is, the Bavarian Illuminati movement ended in 1785. This branch of the movement has since then not recovered. What came of it, died with Adam Weishaupt. The reason as to why you see Illuminati theories everywhere is boredom and projection from society itself.

It's wonderful to think there's some great big conspiracy behind it all, that the select few are crafting your lives and fates as they see fit, that they're the cause of all of our suffering and pain, but that's where the story ends. It's just a fantasy, that a society like that can even exist for real.

Some people go the other way from the fanatics and make jokes about it. The Illuminati memes have been there for years, but they went mainstream around 2005.

Most of them parody conspiracy theorists by taking a popular video and finding triangle shapes in it, then pointing out that the Illuminati put it there, as the triangle eye is their most popular symbol.

The most powerful cult in the world showing its symbol in everyone's face in the most pointless of places, is easy and effective humoring of the Illuminati conspirators. The one-dollar bill pyramid eye being hidden in everything, celebrities doing secret hand gestures and so on, are smart parallels with what the usual Illuminati conspiracy is, it being, they're behind everything, we just don't know it.

You to, can join this funny bandwagon of memes and jokes. It has its funny moments, and just typing in Illuminati on YouTube is enough to find hours of content parodying the belief that the movement exists in the way it does. Or you could go with the side that believes otherwise.

That somehow, these wild stories are real, that they're true. That the Illuminati actually exist. And those people would be fully right. And not just that, numerous Illuminati cults are active all around the world, holding meetings and keeping their eyes on current events. And this isn't another conspiracy theory, this is undeniable truth.

I'll dedicate the final chapter of this book to discussing these organizations. If there are some close to you, maybe you could even join them...

CHAPTER 8

THE LEGACY LIVES ON

One thing is clear, nothing remained of the Bavarian Illuminati. But one thing did remain, and that's reputation. A reputation of wanting what's best for the world, wanting freedom, liberty and logic to rule the day, not morals from ancient books.

These strong Illuminating ideals ring true to this day, as for some people, the world is a very dark and grim place, in need of guidance. This is why all across the world, Illuminati inspired cults exist. What's ironic is that pretty much all of them are publicly known.

What's even more ironic is that they're not publicly known because someone discovered them, but because they advertise themselves online. Cults want and need members, and the modern Illuminati are no exception.

The Illuminati not only exist today, but are so confident in their message that they openly share it with the world. You will find that most countries, if not all, have their own Illuminati-like cults, with some slight differences in their rules and requirements to join them.

It's important to point out that none of them have any historical connection to the Bavarian Illuminati, although many of them say they do. They use this as an effective and smart way to promote their cult.

The cults themselves don't have any actual power, at least on paper.

Nothing stops powerful people from joining their ranks and then using their power to suit some Illuminati goal, but something like this is yet to come up, as joining such a cult deals a very strong and negative impact on one's political reputation.

It's not that people would think that person is a fanatic and shouldn't have influence, it's that they'd think that said person is too nuts for a powerful position.

Another thing that unites them is that all of them have one rule in common, in case you want to join. That you must believe there is a creature far greater and more powerful than us.

That it exists and that its presence is an undeniable constant. This creature doesn't have to be any God, you just have to believe that something wiser and stronger than us exists in the universe.

If you're curious about how your countries Illuminati cult is, the only thing you need to do is type in the name of your country on Google and then add "Join Illuminati" to it.

That should point you in the right direction. So what will your decisions be? Are you ready to join them?

CONCLUSION

No matter how much we look into history, there's always one thing we need to keep in mind. That time and perspective change it. History is said to be written by the victors, and that much is true, but it's also written by liars and jokers.

We can't fully trust any piece of paper fully, but we have too. We're expected too. Because history happened, and we know the truth behind it. We have evidence. Evidence that's mostly badly written pieces of paper and old bones, but evidence nonetheless.

When we're in school, everything we read in the books we're given we take for granted. We take it as unfaultable truth. We accept things like atoms, evolution, DNA and history as facts, even without seeing them with our own eyes.

Without finding out ourselves, without challenging them. Why? Because they're all written down in a fancy, clean book that sounds smart. That sounds sane.

Think about this, if these books said the Bavarian Illuminati were still real and are running the world behind the scenes today... Would you challenge that.....?

Thank you again for purchasing this book!

If you liked this book do you think you could leave me a review on Amazon? Just search for this title and my name on Amazon to find it. Thank you so much!

CHECK OUT MY OTHER BOOKS

Below you'll find some of my other popular books that are popular on Amazon and Kindle as well. You can visit my author page on Amazon to see other work done by me. (Seth Balfour).

True Ghost Stories

UFOs And Aliens

Conspiracy Theories

Missing People

Serial Killers

Cannibal Killers

Missing People – Volume 2

Unexplained Disappearances

Cold Cases True Crime

Haunted Asylums

Haunted Asylums – Volume 2

True Ghost Stories – Volume 2

Women Who Kill

You can simply search for these titles on the Amazon website with my name to find them.

LIBRARY BUGS BOOKS

Like FREE books?

Would you like them delivered to you every week?

Do you like non-fiction books on a huge range of different topics?

We send out FREE e-books every week so we can share our books with the world!

We have FREE books every week on AMAZON that we send to our email list. If you want in, then visit the link below to sign up and sit back and wait for new books to be sent straight to your inbox!

It couldn't be simpler!

www.LibraryBugs.com

If you want FREE books delivered straight to your inbox, then visit the link above and soon you'll be receiving a great list of FREE e-books every week!

Enjoy :)

SETH BALFOUR

Seth Balfour grew up in Los Angeles with a keen eye for crime, murder mysteries and conspiracy theories. Ever since being a kid Seth has studied and dissected many crime stories and twisted conspiracy theories of the world.

The purpose of Seth's books is to reveal the true stories of serial killers, true crime and unsolved mysteries that are talked about in our modern world. The more he reads the more he wants to share with the world his views on crime!

Seth invites you to use his books as a resource and entertainment so that you too can learn of many of the worlds most notorious and well known mysteries of the world. He openly shares everything that he has learned and found intriguing over the years and hopes you find his books interesting and enjoyable.

www.ingramcontent.com/pod-product-compliance
Lightning Source LLC
Chambersburg PA
CBHW030548290526
45786CB00004B/1914